MATH SERIES

Percent

Book design by Kifer Graphics

Copyright © 2000 by Stanley H. Collins

Published by:
Garlic Press
605 Powers St.
Eugene, OR 97402

ISBN 978-0-931993-25-1
Order Number GP-025
Printed in China

www.garlicpress.com

To Parents, Students, and Teachers:

Percent is part of the *Straight Forward Math Series*. Before beginning these percent skills, please make sure that certain pre-learned skills with fractions and decimals are firm. To this end, a simple **Basic Skills Test** for fractions and decimals is placed before the formal introduction of percent. Otherwise, this book is organized to methodically introduce percent concepts and skills. Concepts and skills are explained, modeled, and practiced. Periodic **Review** and **Testing** serve to measure skills taught.

Two other measurement tools–in addition to review and testing–are provided. A **Percent Pre-Test** will survey beginning percent skill levels. A **Percent Post-Test** will measure how well all percent skills presented in the book have been mastered.

Exercises which accompany skill sections can be completed in the book or on separate paper. **Answers** to exercises and all testing are also provided.

These steps are suggested for mastery of percent:

- Give the **Basic Skills Test** (page 6). Basic knowledge and facility with fractions and decimals are prerequisites to the introduction of percent. Without sufficient fraction and decimal knowledge and facility, percent concepts and skills have no firm base.

- Give the **Percent Pre-Test** (page 8). The pre-test is a simple tool to indicate what percent skills a student may already have.

- Proceed with individual skills, starting on page 9. Each skill is explained and modeled. Exercises accompany each skill.

- **Review** is periodically provided as a testing tool.

- Give the **Percent Post-Test** (page 34) as a final measure of skills. Compare the change from the Percent Pre-Test.

Contents

Basic Skills Test 6

Percent Pre-Test 8

    What is Percent? 9
    Percent to Decimal 12
    Decimal to Percent 14
    Percent to Fraction 16
    Fraction to Percent 18

Review 20

    Finding the Part 22
    Finding the Number 24
    Finding the Percent 26
    Word Problems 28

Review 30

    Applying Percent 32

Percent Post-Test 34

Answers 36

Basic Skills Test
for Decimals and Fractions

Equivalent Fractions: Fractions that are the same rational number are equivalent. Fractions can be renamed as equivalent by multiplying and dividing numerators or denominators by the same number.

A. Provide Equivalent Fractions:

$\dfrac{3}{4} =$ 　　　 $\dfrac{5}{6} = \dfrac{}{12} = \dfrac{}{18}$ 　　　 $\dfrac{1}{4} = \dfrac{}{12} = \dfrac{}{16} = \dfrac{}{20}$

$\dfrac{1}{5} =$ 　　　 $\dfrac{2}{3} = \dfrac{}{6} = \dfrac{}{9}$ 　　　 $\dfrac{7}{8} = \dfrac{}{16} = \dfrac{}{24} = \dfrac{}{32}$

$\dfrac{11}{12} =$ 　　　 $\dfrac{25}{100} = \dfrac{}{200} = \dfrac{}{300}$ 　　　 $\dfrac{7}{10} = \dfrac{}{40} = \dfrac{}{50} = \dfrac{}{80}$

B. Provide Equivalent Fractions, reducing to lowest terms when necessary.

$\dfrac{4}{16} = \dfrac{}{12} = \dfrac{}{4}$ 　　 $\dfrac{15}{18} = \dfrac{}{12} = \dfrac{}{6}$ 　　 $\dfrac{25}{75} =$ 　　 $\dfrac{14}{21} =$

$\dfrac{16}{20} = \dfrac{}{10} = \dfrac{}{5}$ 　　 $\dfrac{6}{27} = \dfrac{}{18} = \dfrac{}{9}$ 　　 $\dfrac{10}{14} =$ 　　 $\dfrac{150}{250} =$

$\dfrac{4}{12} = \dfrac{}{6} = \dfrac{}{3}$ 　　 $\dfrac{56}{80} = \dfrac{}{40} = \dfrac{}{20}$ 　　 $\dfrac{8}{18} =$ 　　 $\dfrac{15}{60} =$

C. Operations—Solve the following problems:

$$\begin{array}{r} \dfrac{3}{4} \\[4pt] + \dfrac{5}{6} \\ \hline \end{array} \qquad \begin{array}{r} 23\dfrac{1}{7} \\[4pt] -15\dfrac{2}{3} \\ \hline \end{array} \qquad \dfrac{5}{6} \text{ x } \dfrac{9}{10} =$$

$$\dfrac{5}{6} \div \dfrac{9}{10} = \qquad 12\dfrac{1}{3} + 7\dfrac{7}{15} = \qquad 1\dfrac{4}{9} \div 2\dfrac{1}{2} =$$

Equivalent Fractions and Decimals: Fractions can be expressed as decimals and vice versa.

A. Express these fractions as decimals:

Round to the
<u>nearest thousandth</u>

$\dfrac{9}{10} =$ $\qquad$ $\dfrac{1}{5} =$ $\qquad$ $\dfrac{1}{3} =$

$\dfrac{23}{1000} =$ $\qquad$ $\dfrac{7}{8} =$ $\qquad$ $\dfrac{5}{6} =$

$4\dfrac{57}{100} =$ $\qquad$ $\dfrac{1}{2} =$ $\qquad$ $\dfrac{8}{125} =$

B. Express these decimals as fractions. Reduce as necessary.

.93 $\qquad$ .05 $\qquad$ 5.55

.7 $\qquad$ .125 $\qquad$ 6.025

27.037 $\qquad$ 2.6 $\qquad$ .875

C. Solve the following problems:

42.7 + 8.87 + 7.02 = $\qquad$ 7.62 – 4.9 =

$.5\overline{)10.75}$ $\qquad\qquad$ 6.42
$\qquad\qquad\qquad\qquad\qquad$ x .17
$\qquad\qquad\qquad\qquad\qquad$ ‾‾‾‾‾

$38\overline{)17.1}$ $\qquad\qquad$ $36\overline{)513}$

D. Circle the correct answer:

45 x 9.2 = 414 $\quad$ 4140 $\quad$ 4144.14

26 x .07 = 182 $\quad$ 18.2 $\quad$ 1.82

24.6 x .7 = 17.22 $\quad$ 1722 $\quad$ 172.2

7

Percent Pre-Test

A. Supply the missing equivalents.

	Fraction	**Decimal**	**Percent**
1.	_____	_____	50%
2.	_____	.25	_____
3.	$\dfrac{1}{10}$	_____	_____
4.	_____	.75	_____
5.	_____	_____	45%
6.	$\dfrac{7}{8}$	_____	_____

B. Solve these problems.

1. 80% of 50 =

2. 140% of 20 =

3. 12.5 % of 200 =

4. 10 is 10% of what number?

5. 9 is 72% of what number?

6. 67 is 100% of what number?

7. 20 is what % of 10?

8. What % of $50 is $9.25?

9. 40 is what % of 50?

C. Solve these following word problems.

1. A $95 lamp is discounted 25%. How much is the discount savings?

2. An evening meal totaled $25. If a 5% tip is included, how much is spent for the meal and tip?

3. What is an 11% commission for a $2600 sale?

4. What is the cost of a $35 sweater on sale for 40% off?

What is Percent?

Percent means *part of 100* and is represented by this symbol, %.

100% is equivalent to $\frac{100}{100}$, one hundred parts of 100.

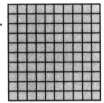

$\frac{100 \text{ parts}}{\text{of } 100}$

•Less than 1 Whole

Percent can name quantities less than 1 whole; that is, less than 100%.

For Example:

27%   98%   33.3%
27 parts   98 parts   33.3 parts
of 100   of 100   of 100

•Greater than 1 Whole

Percent can name quantities greater than 1 whole; that is, greater than 100%.

For Example:

        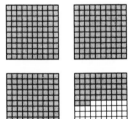   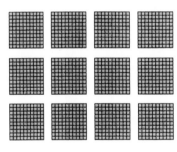

120%   353%   1200%
1 whole, 20 parts   3 whole, 53 parts   12 whole, no parts
of 100   of 100

Exercise 1: What is Percent? Rewrite these percents as a whole number and/or parts of 100.

1. 12% = _____ parts of 100.

2. 35% = _____ parts of 100.

3. 4% = _____ parts of 100.

4. 25.4% = _____ parts of 100.

5. 66.666% = _____ parts of 100.

6. 536% = _____ whole, _____ parts of 100.

7. 1000% = _____ whole, _____ parts of 100.

8. 1720% = _____ whole, _____ parts of 100.

9. 5010% = _____ whole, _____ parts of 100.

10. 920.5% = _____ whole, _____ parts of 100.

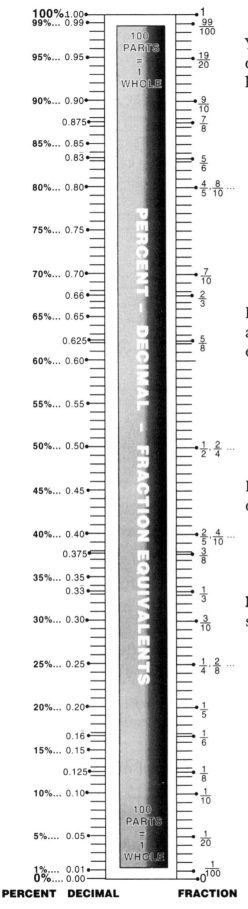

You have already learned that fractions and decimals are different methods for naming numbers and you have learned that fractions and decimals have equivalents.

For Example:
$$15.5 = 15\frac{1}{2}$$
$$.7 = \frac{7}{10}$$
$$.25 = \frac{1}{4}$$
$$29.33\overline{3} = 29\frac{1}{3}$$

Percent is also a way to name a number. When a fraction, a decimal, or a percent names the same number, they are equivalent.

For Example: $\frac{1}{2}$, .50 , 50%

All name the same quantity,
only their written form is different.

If we construct a Number Line (see left column), fractions, decimals, and percents more easily show their equivalence.

Exercise 2: What is Percent? Using the Number Line, supply the two missing equivalents:

	Fraction	**Decimal**	**Percent**
1.	_____	.5	_____
2.	_____	.4	_____
3.	_____	_____	25%
4.	$\frac{1}{8}$	_____	_____
5.	_____	1	_____

10

	Fraction	Decimal	Percent
6.	_____	_____	75%
7.	_____	.10	_____
8.	$\frac{1}{20}$	_____	_____
9.	_____	_____	1%
10.	$\frac{1}{5}$	_____	_____

Exercise 3: What is Percent? Review. Shade the correct parts of 100 which are equivalent to the given percent.

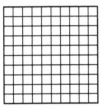   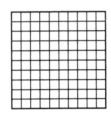   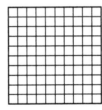   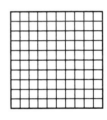

   32%   17%   98%   80%

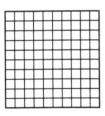   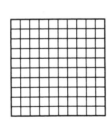   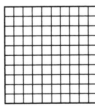   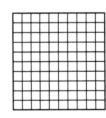

   6%   64%   44%   1%

   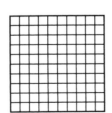   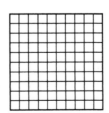

   152%   108%

Percent to Decimal

Rule: To convert from a percent to a decimal, drop the percent sign (%) and move the decimal point two places to the left. Insert zeros when necessary.

Examples:

.8% = .8 = .008

3% = 3 = .03

5.2% = 5.2 = .052

18% = 18 = .18

17.2% = 17.2 = .172

115% = 115 = 1.15

5000% = 5000 = 50

Exercise 1: Percent to a Decimal. Convert each percent to a decimal.

1. 68%   **2.** 5%   **3.** 25.8%

4. 1%   **5.** 99.9%   **6.** .06%

7. 225%   **8.** 7000%   **9.** 1528%

10. 5.529%   **11.** .9%   **12.** 52.47%

13. 7.6%   **14.** 172%   **15.** 49.06%

16. 453.1%   **17.** 67%   **18.** .5%

•Percents with Fractions

Percents that include fractions can be converted into decimals, too:

1. Change the fraction into its decimal equivalent;
2. Place a decimal point before the new equivalent;
3. Proceed with the conversion rule.

Examples: $12\frac{2}{5}\%$ = 12.40 = 12.4 0 = .124

$6\frac{3}{8}\%$ = 6.375 = 6.3 7 5 = .06375

$11\frac{1}{20}\%$ = 11.05 = 11.0 5 = .1105

Exercise 2: Percent to Decimal. Convert each percent to a decimal.

1. .6%

2. 122%

3. 427.5%

4. .001%

5. $5\frac{1}{20}\%$

6. 4000%

7. $8\frac{1}{2}\%$

8. 19.03%

9. 5.722%

10. 85%

11. $43\frac{1}{10}\%$

12. 23.47%

13. $230\frac{1}{8}\%$

14. 1200%

15. .245%

16. 1600.5%

17. $37\frac{3}{5}\%$

18. 17%

19. 11.01%

20. 8.297%

21. $3\frac{3}{4}\%$

Decimal to Percent

Rule: To convert from a decimal to a percent, move the decimal point two places to the right and add a percent (%) sign. Insert zeros when necessary.

Examples:

$.02 = .02 = 2\%$

$.4 = .4 = 40\%$

$.37 = .37 = 37\%$

$6 = 6. = 600\%$

$9.5 = 9.5 = 950\%$

$12.46 = 12.46 = 1246\%$

$.064 = .064 = 6.4\%$

Exercise 1: Decimal to Percent. Convert each decimal to a percent.

1. 88

2. .7

3. .31

4. .201

5. .09

6. .016

7. 7.3

8. 18.32

9. .541

10. 6.712

11. 1.4

12. .618

13. .0215

14. .178

15. 24.6

16. 5

17. 4.01

18. .003

Exercise 2: Decimal to Percent. Convert each decimal to a percent.

1. .038   2. .014   3. .04

4. .02   5. .47   6. .85

7. .643   8. .307   9. .005

Exercise 3: Decimal to Percent. Circle the correct percent equivalent.

1. .0678	=	.678%	6.78%	67.8%
2. 7	=	7%	70%	700%
3. 1.4	=	1.4%	14%	140%
4. .6	=	60%	6%	.6%
5. 32.75	=	327.5%	3275%	32750%
6. 1.82	=	1820%	182%	18.2%
7. 39	=	3900%	390%	3.90%
8. .5987	=	5.987%	59.87%	598.7%
9. 6.4 + 2.3	=	87%	870%	neither
10. 14.5 – 7.6	=	69%	6.9%	neither

Percent to Fraction

Rule: To convert from a percent to a fraction, remove the percent sign (%) and place the number over a denominator of 100. Reduce to lowest terms, if necessary.

Examples:

$3\% = \dfrac{3}{100}$

$80\% = \dfrac{80}{100} = \dfrac{4}{5}$

$64\% = \dfrac{64}{100} = \dfrac{32}{50} = \dfrac{16}{25}$

$125\% = \dfrac{125}{100} = 1\dfrac{25}{100} = 1\dfrac{1}{4}$

$1250\% = \dfrac{1250}{100} = 12\dfrac{50}{100} = 12\dfrac{1}{2}$

Exercise 1: Percent to Fraction. Convert each percent to a fraction. Reduce fractions to lowest terms.

1. 75%   **2.** 2%   **3.** 6%

4. 57%   **5.** 64%   **6.** 93%

7. 120%   **8.** 88%   **9.** 250%

10. 500%   **11.** 1430%   **12.** 5%

13. 60%   **14.** 70%   **15.** 105%

16. 325%   **17.** 95%   **18.** 100%

Further Examples:

$$18.6\% = \frac{18.6}{100} = \frac{186}{1000} = \frac{93}{500}$$

$$3.09\% = \frac{3.09}{100} = \frac{309}{10000}$$

$$12\frac{3}{4}\% = \frac{\frac{51}{4}}{100} = \frac{\frac{51}{4} \times 4}{100 \times 4} = \frac{51}{400}$$

or

$$12.75\% = \frac{12.75}{100} = \frac{1275}{10000} = \frac{51}{400}$$

$$\frac{2}{3}\% = \frac{\frac{2}{3}}{100} = \frac{\frac{2}{3} \times 3}{100 \times 3} = \frac{2}{300} = \frac{1}{150}$$

$$33\frac{1}{3}\% = \frac{33\frac{1}{3}}{100} = \frac{\frac{100}{3}}{100} = \frac{\frac{100}{3} \times 3}{100 \times 3} = \frac{100}{300} = \frac{1}{3}$$

Exercise 2: Percent to Fraction. Convert each percent to a fraction. Reduce fractions to lowest terms.

1. .407%

2. 60.1%

3. 17.3%

4. 54.9%

5. 17.75%

6. 55.25%

7. 94.75%

8. 72.4%

9. 2.375%

10. 15.5%

11. $\frac{1}{2}$ %

12. $\frac{2}{3}$ %

13. $60\frac{3}{5}$ %

14. $12\frac{1}{4}$ %

15. $65\frac{1}{2}$ %

16. $70\frac{1}{5}$ %

17. $2\frac{3}{4}$ %

18. $8\frac{1}{3}$ %

19. $13\frac{1}{2}$ %

20. $24\frac{2}{5}$ %

21. $4\frac{1}{10}$ %

Fraction to Percent

Rule: To convert from a fraction to a percent: 1) convert any mixed number to an improper fraction; 2) divide the numerator of the fraction by its denominator; 3) multiply by 100 (or simply move the decimal point 2 places to the right); 4) add a percent (%) sign.

Examples:

$$\frac{5}{8} \quad = \quad 5 \div 8 \quad = \quad .625 \times 100 \quad = \quad 62.5\%$$

or

$$\frac{5}{8} \quad = \quad 5 \div 8 \quad = \quad .6\,2\,5 \quad = \quad 62.5\%$$

$$\frac{5}{16} \quad = \quad 5 \div 16 \quad = \quad .3\,1\,2\,5 \quad = \quad 31.25\%$$

$$\frac{24}{100} \quad \text{if denominator} \quad = \quad 100 \quad = \quad .24\%$$

$$\frac{3.5}{100} \quad = \quad \frac{35}{1000} \quad = \quad 35 \div 1000 \quad = \quad .0\,3\,5 \quad = \quad 3.5\%$$

$$3\frac{2}{5} \quad = \quad \frac{17}{5} \quad = \quad 17 \div 5 \quad = \quad 3.\,4 \quad = \quad 340\%$$

$$8 \quad \text{no divison necessary} \quad = \quad 8 \quad = \quad 800\%$$

Exercise 1. Fraction to Percent. Convert each fraction to a percent.

1. $\dfrac{49}{100}$

2. $\dfrac{13}{100}$

3. $\dfrac{3.2}{100}$

4. $\dfrac{1}{2}$

5. $\dfrac{3}{4}$

6. $\dfrac{3}{5}$

7. $\dfrac{9}{20}$

8. $\dfrac{8}{25}$

9. $\dfrac{1}{10}$

10. $\dfrac{27}{40}$

11. 12

12. $\dfrac{51}{75}$

13. $2\dfrac{4}{5}$

14. $\dfrac{25.75}{100}$

15. $1\dfrac{1}{2}$

Exercice 2.   Fraction to Percent. Convert each fraction to a percent. Round any repeating decimals to the nearest hundredth before converting to a percent.

1. $\frac{19}{100}$

2. $\frac{7}{18}$

3. $\frac{0.73}{100}$

4. $\frac{7}{4}$

5. $3\frac{3}{5}$

6. $\frac{9}{8}$

7. $\frac{1}{3}$

8. 4

9. $\frac{9}{50}$

10. $\frac{318}{10,000}$

11. $\frac{2}{3}$

12. $\frac{16}{12}$

13. $\frac{11}{30}$

14. $\frac{3}{16}$

15. $\frac{1}{4}$

16. $\frac{18}{5}$

17. $\frac{5}{6}$

18. $\frac{1}{8}$

19. $4\frac{1}{7}$

20. $9\frac{4}{9}$

21. $7\frac{13}{20}$

Review

A. Convert each percent to a decimal.

    1. 726%   **2.** 3%   **3.** 27.2%

    4. 6.99%   **5.** 12.5%   **6.** .09%

    7. 2275%   **8.** $24\frac{3}{5}$ %   **9.** $3\frac{1}{8}$ %

B. Convert each decimal to a percent.

    1. .07   **2.** .472   **3.** 7.6

    4. 6   **5.** .0028   **6.** .0876

    7. .8   **8.** 15   **9.** .72

C. Convert each percent to a fraction. Reduce to lowest terms if necessary.

    1. 55%   **2.** 800%   **3.** 7%

    4. 90%   **5.** $12\frac{1}{4}$ %   **6.** $\frac{1}{2}$%

    7. 6.2%   **8.** $5\frac{1}{10}$ %   **9.** 1.125%

D. Convert each fraction to a percent. Round any repeating decimal to the nearest hundredth.

    1. $\frac{1}{3}$ **2.** $\frac{1}{2}$ **3.** $3\frac{3}{5}$

    4. 12   **5.** $\frac{8}{7}$ **6.** $10\frac{5}{6}$

    7. $\frac{11}{20}$ **8.** $\frac{21}{6}$ **9.** $\frac{.75}{100}$

E. Use equivalent forms to complete this table:

	Percent	Decimal	Fraction
1.	25%	_____	_____
2.	_____	.04	_____
3.	_____	_____	$\frac{1}{8}$
4.	_____	.32	_____
5.	50%	_____	_____
6.	_____	_____	$\frac{4}{5}$
7.	37%	_____	_____
8.	_____	_____	$\frac{16}{25}$
9.	125%	_____	_____
10.	_____	.001	_____
11.	$7\frac{1}{2}$%	_____	_____
12.	_____	_____	$7\frac{3}{4}$
13.	_____	.035	_____
14.	4.5%	_____	_____
15.	_____	_____	$\frac{1}{16}$
16.	167.5%	_____	_____
17.	$\frac{3}{5}$%	_____	_____
18.	_____	_____	8
19.	_____	.745	_____
20.	.6%	_____	_____

Finding the Part

Many problems that use percent require us to solve for one of three variables: a part of a whole number, a whole number, or a percent of a whole number. We begin here with a typical form for *Finding the Part* of a whole number:

15% of 60 is what number?   In written mathematical form.

15% of 60 =   In simpler mathematical form.

A very simple formula will help solve, in this case, for the missing part, but it will also help us later to solve for one of the other variables: a missing whole number, or a missing percent.

Part (**P**art) = Percent (**R**ate) x Whole Number (**N**umber)
P = R x N

Example: 15% of 60 is what number?

15% x 60 =	From written form to mathematical form.
15%(**R**) x 60 (**N**) = P	Identify variables.
P = 15% x 60	
P = .15 x 60	Change the percent to a decimal. Multiply.
P = 9	Answer: **9** is 15% of 60

Exercise 1: Finding the Part. Find the part of these wholes.

1. 80% of 50   **2.** 6% of 56   **3.** 25% of 8

4. 95% of 62   **5.** 15% of 140   **6.** 32% of 150

7. 140% of 20   **8.** 18.5% of 50   **9.** 104% of 120

10. 12.5% of 200   **11.** $\frac{3}{4}$% of 6   **12.** 7.5% of 830

•Two Forms

Problems which require you to find the part can be written in two forms:

What is (=) 15% of (x) 60?

or

15% of (x) 60 is (=) what number?

Both ways translate into the mathematical form of:

15% x 60 = ?

And both mathematical forms fit our formula of **P = R x N**.

Exercise 2: Finding the Part: Solve these problems which use the two forms:

1. 20% of 18 is what number?

2. What number is 45% of 30?

3. What number is 1.6% of 85?

4. 3.5% of 78 is what number?

5. .052% of 30 is what number?

6. What number is $8\frac{1}{2}$ % of 100?

7. What is 60% of $15\frac{1}{2}$?

8. 130% of 150 is what number?

9. What number is 6% of 9.6?

10. 46.9% of 1.8 is what number?

11. 100% of 27.4 is what number?

12. What number is $17\frac{1}{4}$ % of 150?

13. What number is 2.2% of 15?

14. What number is 6.5% of 200?

Finding the Number

A second variable that percent problems often require us to find is the Number. The typical *Find the Number* form is:

48 is 60% of what number?

Translating the written form into a more compact mathematical form gives us:

48 = 60% x N

Remember the formula **P = R** x **N**. In the example above, the **P**art (48) is known and the **R**ate (60%) is known, but the **N**umber **(N)** is unknown.

To solve for the **N**umber, the formula is adjusted to:

$$N = \frac{P}{R}$$

Example: 48 = 60% x N

48(P) = 60% (R) x N   Identify the variables.

$$N = \frac{48 \ (P)}{.6 \ (R)}$$ Isolate the unknown. Divide.

N = 80   Answer: **80** equals 60% of 48.

Exercise 1: Finding the Number. Find the Number for the following problems:

1. 10 is 10% of what number?

2. 50 is $33\frac{1}{3}$% of what number?

3. 20 is 200% of what number?

4. 26.5 is 50% of what number?

5. 150 is 25% of what number?

6. 19 is 19% of what number?

7. 9 is 72% of what number?

8. 67 is 100% of what number?

9. 84 is 35% of what number?

10. 42 is 70% of what number?

Exercise 2: Finding the Number. Solve the following Problems. Converting any fractions to decimals may aid in a quicker solution.

1. $1.35 is 18% of what number?

2. 90 is 72% of what number?

3. 66 is 1.5% of what number?

4. 3.8 is 16% of what number?

5. 84 is 120% of what number?

6. $5\frac{5}{8}$ is 30% of what number?

7. .008 is .025% of what number?

8. $12.98 is 22% of what number?

9. 44 is 80% of what number?

10. 1.8 is .06% of what number?

11. $39\frac{1}{2}$ is 25% of what number?

12. 27 is 75% of what number?

13. 8.84 is 52% of what number?

14. 45 is $62\frac{1}{2}$% of what number?

15. $32.75 is 1% of what number?

16. $40.81 is 77% of what number?

Finding the Percent

A third variable that percent problems often require us to find is the Percent. The typical *Find the Percent* form is:

8 is what % of 25?

or

What % of 25 is 8?

Translating the written form into mathematical form gives us:

8 = what % x 25

What % x 25 = 8

Remember the formula **P** = **R** x **N**. In case above, the **P**art (8) is known and the **N**umber (25) is known, but the Percent (**R**) is unknown.

To solve for the percent (**R**), the formula is adjusted to:

$$\mathbf{R} = \frac{\mathbf{P}}{\mathbf{B}}$$

Example:

8 = _____% x 25

8(P) = (R) x 25(N)   Identify the variables.

$$R = \frac{8\ \mathbf{(P)}}{25\ \mathbf{(N)}}$$ Isolate the unknown. Divide.

R = .32 = 32%   Answer: 8 is **32%** of 48.

Exercise 1: Finding the Percent. Find the Number for the following:

1. 20 is what % of 10?   **2.** 24 is what % of 40?

3. What % of 60 is 45?   **4.** What % of 7.5 is 3?

5. $1\frac{1}{2}$ is what % of 50?   **6.** 1.3 is what % of 6.50?

7. What % of 46 is 17.94?   **8.** $9.25 is what % of $50.00?

9. What % of 20 is 28?   **10.** What % of 76 is 8.93?

Exercise 2: Finding the Percent. Solve the following Problems.

1. What % of 200 is 25?

2. 124.8 is what % of 120?

3. 150 is what % of 32?

4. What % of 84 is 21?

5. What % of $18 is $3.60?

6. 9.3 is what % of 15.5?

7. 3.3 is what % of 1.5?

8. What % of 1500 is 1905?

9. $2.73 is what % of $78?

10. 90 is what % of 300?

11. What % of 50 is $30\frac{1}{2}$?

12. What % of $2\frac{2}{3}$ is $\frac{8}{15}$?

13. 72 is what % of 28.8?

14. What % of $12\frac{1}{2}$ is 12?

15. $4\frac{1}{8}$ is % of $6\frac{7}{8}$?

16. 1.3 is what % of 6.5?

Word Problems

You have learned three variations of one formula to solve percent problems:

$$P = R \times N \qquad \text{Part} = \text{Rate} \times \text{Number}$$

$$N = \frac{P}{R} \qquad \text{Number} = \text{Part} \div \text{Rate}$$

$$R = \frac{P}{N} \qquad \text{Rate} = \text{Part} \div \text{Number}$$

Consider how these three formulas are used in word problems:

Example 1: $P = R \times N$

80% of 20 is what number?

Word Problem: How many questions must Elena answer correctly (P) to receive 80% (R) on a 20-item test (N)?

Example 2: $N = \frac{P}{R}$

16 is 80% of what number?

Word Problem: Elena answered 16 questions (P) correctly on a test and received a score of 80% (R). How many questions (N) were on the test?

Example 3: $R = \frac{P}{N}$

16 is what % of 20?

Word Problem: Elena correctly answers 16 questions (P) out of 20 (N) test questions. What percent (R) were answered correctly.

Exercise 1: Word Problems. Use the three formulas to solve the following word problems.

1. A local college has an enrollment of 3500 students (N). 30% of the students (R) live on campus. How many students live on campus?

2. Suppose 120 students (P) out of 150 (N) purchased special movie tickets. What percent (R) is that?

3. Emily spent $45 (P) of her savings. This is 25% (R) of her total savings (N). How much was her total savings?

4. A shirt originally selling for $37.50 (N) was reduced to $26.25 (P) on sale. What percent (R) of the original price is the sale price?

5. A sales tax rate of 5% (R) gives $1.50 (P) on what purchase amount (N)?

6. Four pairs of sox cost $19.80 (N). The sales tax is 5% (R). How much is the sales tax?

7. In a local election, 208 people out of 320 possible voters cast ballots. What percent cast ballots?

8. 15% of the students in school eat hot lunch. If 108 have hot lunch, how many students attend the school?

9. Jane spent 26% of her monthly $3400 salary on rent. How much did she spend on monthly rent?

10. A ball team won 9 of 15 games. What percent of games did the team win?

11. A customer received .057% interest on her $400 savings account. How much interest was paid on the $400?

12. A 10% interest payment increased Juan's bank account by $14.80. How much money did Juan have in his account to receive $14.80 in interest?

Review

A. Complete each of the following:

1. 27 is 75% of _____

2. 29 is _____% of 116

3. What percent of 7.5 is 3?

4. 12 is 12% of _____

5. 17% of 190 = _____

6. 45 is _____% of 75

7. 8.48 is 53% of _____

8. 15.8% of 72 = _____

9. 68 is 200% of _____

10. $62\frac{1}{2}$% of 96 = _____

11. 56 is $87\frac{1}{2}$% of _____

12. 18.36 is _____% of 72

13. $37\frac{1}{2}$% of 88 = _____

14. 475 is 190% of _____

15. 124 is what % of 1240?

16. $66\frac{2}{3}$% of 96 is _____

17. 17.02 is 46% of _____

18. 52.8 is _____% of 75

19. 15% of 15 is _____

20. 53.2% of 29 equals _____

B. Solve each word problem:

1. A mountain bike normally sells for $295. If the original price is reduced by $50.15, what is the percent of savings?

2. The sale price of a pair of shoes is $21. The sale price is 70% of the regular price. What is the regular price?

3. If an item normally costs $225 and it is offered at a 30% discount, how much will the discount be?

C. Solve the following problems:

1. 42.5% of 230 is what number?

2. What number is 12.5% of 178?

3. 88 is what percent of 64?

4. 1067.5 is 250% of what number?

5. 63 is what percent of 300?

6. 386 is 19.3% of what number?

Applying Percent

Here are problems that illustrate common applications of percent. These applications most frequently occur in our day-to-day lives.

Example 1: Taxes-Tipping-Commissions

- •Taxes: A $249 sofa has a 5% sales tax. How much is the tax?
Tax (P) = .05 (R) x $249 (N)
Tax = $12.45

- •Tipping: The luncheon bill from a company meeting was $275.50. The restaurant requires a 12% gratuity (tip) for this size of meeting. How much was the tip?
Tip = .12 x $275.50
Tip = $33.06

- •Commission: A salesperson earns 11% on all sales she makes. Last week she sold $3200 worth of goods. What was her commission for the week?
Commission = .11 x $3200
Commission = $352.00

Example 2: Discounts-Sales Prices

- •Discounts: A stylish coat is advertised on sale at a 20% discount. The regular price is $150. Find the discount.
Discount = .20 x $150
Discount = $30

- •Sale Prices: A stylish coat is advertised on sale at a 20% discount. The regular price is $150. Find the sale price.
Method 1-2 steps:
Step 1: D = .20 x $150   Step 2: Regular price − Discount = Sale Price
          D = $30 $150 − $30 = Sale Price
                                                  $120 = Sale Price

Method 2-1 step:
Sale Price = $150 x .80   .80 = 100% (original percent) − 20% (sale percent)
Sale Price = $120

  Note : This 1-step method can also be applied to tax, tipping, and commission problems.

  A $249 sofa has a 5% sales tax. What is the total cost including the sales tax?

  Total: Cost + tax = 1.05 x $249   1.05 = 100% (cost price) + 5% (sales tax)
  Total: Cost + tax = $261.45

Exercise 1: Applying Percent. Solve each problem. Use the 1-Step Method whenever possible.

1. A $45 camera is discounted 25%. How much is the discount savings? What is the discounted price of the camera?

2. A car salesperson receives a 9% commission on all cars he sells. If he sells a car for $4500, what is his commission?

3. Cab fare to the International Airport is $17.50. If the cab driver is tipped 20%, what is the tip amount?

4. A sweater that originally sold for $35 is marked down 15%. What is the savings? What is the sales price?

5. A machinist making $18.50 per hour receives an 8% raise. What is the new hourly wage?

6. A salesperson sold a $350 chair, a $295 stove, and a $179 rug. What is her commission on all items at a 12% rate?

7. What is the tax at a 5.5% rate on an expensive car costing $24,520?

8. The salesperson in Problem 7 received an 8.5% commission on the sale. How much was the commission, tax not included?

9. A clothing store advertised a 30% savings on all clothes purchased. If you plan to purchase $928 in clothing, what is your savings? What will you finally pay?

10. A salesperson was very helpful. She was able to get a 20% discount for a customer on a $1250 item. She also received a 7% commission on the sale. What was the sale price of the item? What was the salesperson's commission on the item?

Percent Post-Test

A. Supply equivalent values:

	Fraction	Decimal	Percent
1.	$\frac{1}{8}$	_____	_____
2.	_____	_____	120%
3.	_____	.055	_____
4.	$\frac{3}{500}$	_____	_____
5.	_____	7.9	_____
6.	_____	_____	5%
7.	_____	_____	1250%
8.	_____	4.375	_____
9.	$\frac{7}{4}$	_____	_____
10.	_____	.0625	_____

B. Solve the following problems:

1. 125 is $33\frac{1}{3}$% of what number?

2. What percent of 60 is 45?

3. 325% of 50 equals what number?

4. $17\frac{1}{4}$% of 150 is what number?

5. $12.75 is 60% of what number?

6. 2.5 is what percent of 40?

7. What number is 27% of 10?

8. 80 is 128% of what number?

9. $6.25 is what percent of $25?

10. What number is .09% of 52?

C. Word problems.

  1. On a 50-question test, Danielle answered 78% of the questions correctly. How many questions did she answer correctly?

  2. Four pairs of sox cost $5.50. A 6% sales tax was added. How much was the purchase including the sales tax?

  3. A local grocery store handed out 2470 coupons for a reduced price on detergent. 1482 coupons were returned. What percent of the coupons were returned?

  4. A $45 appliance was purchased on sale at a 30% discount. What was the price of the appliance after the discount?

  5. Of the employees at a large corporation, 14% filed their income tax reports late. If 168 people filed late tax reports, how many people are employed at the corporation?

  6. Twenty-six out of 160 people who answered a newspaper ad were not qualified for the advertised job. What percent of those answering the ad were not qualified?

  7. Daphne spent her $210 budget on Christmas gifts. This amount was 30% of her savings. How much was her savings?

  8. What is a 15.5% tip on a $120 meal?

  9. A pair of skis is priced at $185. Find the cost including a sales tax of 8%. Find the cost with a discount of 10% and a sales tax of 8%.

  10. The senior class raised 98% of its goal for graduation activities. It raised $10,878. How much was its goal?

  11. The sales tax on a new car is $979.60. The car sold for $15,800. What is the sales tax rate?

  12. Cecily saves 6% of her salary. If she saves $900 in one year, what is her annual salary?

ANSWERS

Basic Slills Test, pages 6–7.

Equivalent Fractions: Fractions that are the same rational number are equivalent. Fractions can be renamed as equivalent by multiplying and dividing numerators or denominators by the same number.

A. Provide Equivalent Equations:

$\frac{3}{4} = \frac{\mathbf{6}}{\mathbf{8}}$ May vary. $\frac{5}{6} = \frac{\mathbf{10}}{\mathbf{12}} = \frac{\mathbf{15}}{18}$ $\frac{1}{4} = \frac{\mathbf{3}}{12} = \frac{\mathbf{4}}{16} = \frac{\mathbf{5}}{20}$

$\frac{1}{5} = \frac{\mathbf{2}}{\mathbf{10}}$ May vary. $\frac{2}{3} = \frac{\mathbf{4}}{6} = \frac{\mathbf{6}}{9}$ $\frac{7}{8} = \frac{\mathbf{14}}{16} = \frac{\mathbf{21}}{24} = \frac{\mathbf{28}}{32}$

$\frac{11}{12} = \frac{\mathbf{22}}{\mathbf{24}}$ May vary. $\frac{25}{100} = \frac{\mathbf{50}}{200} = \frac{\mathbf{75}}{300}$ $\frac{7}{10} = \frac{\mathbf{28}}{40} = \frac{\mathbf{35}}{50} = \frac{\mathbf{56}}{80}$

B. Provide Equivalent Fractions reduced to lowest terms:

$\frac{4}{16} = \frac{\mathbf{3}}{12} = \frac{\mathbf{1}}{4}$ $\frac{15}{18} = \frac{\mathbf{10}}{12} = \frac{\mathbf{5}}{6}$ $\frac{25}{75} = \frac{\mathbf{1}}{\mathbf{3}}$ $\frac{14}{21} = \frac{\mathbf{2}}{\mathbf{3}}$

$\frac{16}{20} = \frac{\mathbf{8}}{\mathbf{10}} = \frac{\mathbf{4}}{\mathbf{5}}$ $\frac{6}{27} = \frac{\mathbf{4}}{18} = \frac{\mathbf{2}}{9}$ $\frac{10}{14} = \frac{\mathbf{5}}{\mathbf{7}}$ $\frac{150}{250} = \frac{\mathbf{3}}{\mathbf{5}}$

$\frac{4}{12} = \frac{\mathbf{2}}{6} = \frac{\mathbf{1}}{3}$ $\frac{56}{80} = \frac{\mathbf{28}}{40} = \frac{\mathbf{14}}{20}$ $\frac{8}{18} = \frac{\mathbf{4}}{\mathbf{9}}$ $\frac{15}{60} = \frac{\mathbf{1}}{\mathbf{4}}$

C. Operations: solve the following problems:

$\begin{array}{r} \frac{3}{4} \\ + \frac{5}{6} \\ \hline \mathbf{1\frac{7}{12}} \end{array}$ $\begin{array}{r} 23\frac{1}{7} \\ -15\frac{2}{3} \\ \hline \mathbf{7\frac{10}{21}} \end{array}$ $\frac{5}{6} \times \frac{9}{10} = \mathbf{\frac{3}{4}}$

$\frac{5}{6} + \frac{9}{10} = \mathbf{\frac{25}{27}}$ $12\frac{1}{3} + 7\frac{7}{15} = \mathbf{19\frac{4}{5}}$ $1\frac{4}{9} + 2\frac{1}{2} = \mathbf{\frac{26}{45}}$

Equivalent Fractions and Decimals: Fractions can be expressed as decimals and vice versa.

A. Express these fractions as decimals: Round to the nearest thousandth

$\frac{9}{10} = \mathbf{.9}$ $\frac{1}{5} = \mathbf{.2}$ $\frac{1}{3} = \mathbf{.33\bar{3}} = \mathbf{.333}$

$\frac{23}{1000} = \mathbf{.023}$ $\frac{7}{8} = \mathbf{.875}$ $\frac{5}{6} = \mathbf{.83\bar{3}} = \mathbf{.833}$

$4\frac{57}{100} = \mathbf{4.57}$ $\frac{1}{2} = \mathbf{.5}$ $\frac{8}{125} = \mathbf{.064}$

B. Express these decimals as fractions. Reduce as necessary.

$.93 = \mathbf{\frac{93}{100}}$ $.05 = \mathbf{\frac{1}{20}}$ $5.55 = \mathbf{5\frac{11}{20}}$

$.7 = \mathbf{\frac{7}{10}}$ $.125 = \mathbf{\frac{1}{8}}$ $6.024 = \mathbf{6\frac{1}{40}}$

$27.037 = \mathbf{27\frac{37}{100}}$ $2.6 = \mathbf{2\frac{3}{5}}$ $.875 = \mathbf{\frac{7}{8}}$

C. Solve the following problems:

$42.7 + 8.87 + 7.02 = \mathbf{58.59}$ $7.62 - 4.9 = \mathbf{2.72}$

$.5\overline{)10.75}\;\; \mathbf{21.5}$ $\begin{array}{r} 6.42 \\ \times\, .17 \\ \hline \mathbf{1.0914} \end{array}$

$38\overline{)17.1}\;\; \mathbf{.45}$ $36\overline{)513}\;\; \mathbf{14.25}$

D. Circle the correct answer:

$45 \times 9.2 =$ (**414**) 4140 4144.14

$26 \times .07 =$ 182 18.2 (**1.82**)

$24.6 \times .7 =$ (**17.22**) 1722 172.2

Percent Pre-Test, page 8.

A. Supply the missing equivalents.

Fraction	Decimal	Percent
1. $\frac{1}{2}$	.5	50%
2. $\frac{1}{4}$	.25	**25%**
3. $\frac{1}{10}$	.1	10%
4. $\frac{3}{4}$	.75	**75%**
5. $\frac{9}{20}$	**.45**	45%
6. $\frac{7}{8}$	**.875**	**87.5%**

B. Solve these problems.

1. 80% of 50 = **40**   4. 10 is 10% of what number? **100**   7. 20 is what % of 10? **200%**

2. 140% of 20 = **28**   5. 9 is 72% of what number? **12.5**   8. What % of $50 is $9.25? **18.5%**

3. 12.5 % of 200 = **25**   6. 67 is 100% of what number? **67**   9. 40 is what % of 50? **80%**

C. Solve these following word problems.

1. A $95 lamp is discounted 25%. How much is the discount savings?
$23.75
2. An evening meal totaled $25. If a 5% tip is included, how much is spent for the meal and tip?
$26.25
3. What is an 11% commission for a $2600 sale?
$286
4. What is the cost of a $35 sweater on sale for 40% off?
$21.00

Exercise 1: What is Percent? page 9.

1. 12% = **12** parts of 100.
2. 35% = **35** parts of 100.
3. 4% = **4** parts of 100.
4. 25.4% = **25.4** parts of 100.
5. 66.666% = **66.666** parts of 100.
6. 536% = **5** whole, **36** parts of 100.
7. 1000% = **10** whole, **0** parts of 100.
8. 1720% = **17** whole, **20** parts of 100.
9. 5010% = **50** whole, **10** parts of 100.
10. 920.5% = **9** whole, **20** parts of 100.

Exercise 2: What is Percent? page 10–11.

	Fraction	Decimal	Percent
1.	$\frac{1}{2}$	.5	**50%**
2.	$\frac{2}{5}$	.4	40%
3.	$\frac{1}{4}$	.25	25%
4.	$\frac{1}{8}$	.125	**12.5%**
5.	1	1	**100%**
6.	$\frac{3}{4}$	.75	75%
7.	$\frac{1}{10}$	.10	**10%**
8.	$\frac{1}{20}$	.05	**5%**
9.	$\frac{1}{100}$	.01	1%
10.	$\frac{1}{5}$	.2	**20%**

36

Exercise 3: What is Percent, page 11.

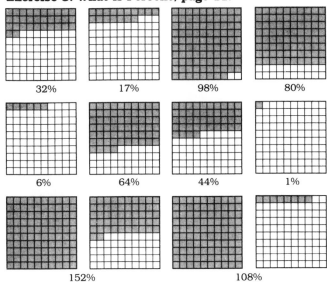

32%	17%	98%	80%
6%	64%	44%	1%

152%   108%

Exercise 3: Decimal to Percent, page 15.

1. .0678	=	.678%	(6.78%)	67.8%
2. 7	=	7%	70%	(700%)
3. 1.4	=	1.4%	14%	(140%)
4. .6	=	(60%)	6%	.6%
5. 32.75	=	327.5%	(3275%)	32750%
6. 1.82	=	1820%	(182%)	18.2%
7. 39	=	(3900%)	390%	3.90%
8. .5987	=	5.987%	(59.87%)	598.7%
9. 6.4 + 2.3	=	87%	(870%)	neither
10. 14.5 – 7.6	=	69%	6.9%	(neither)

Exercise 1: Percent to Decimal, page 12.

1. .68	**2.** .05	**3.** .258
4. .01	**5.** .999	**6.** .0006
7. 2.25	**8.** 70	**9.** 15.28
10. .05529	**11.** .009	**12.** .5247
13. .076	**14.** 1.72	**15.** .4906
16. 4.531	**17.** .67	**18.** .005

Exercise 2: Percent to Decimal, page 13.

1. .006	**2.** 1.22	**3.** 4.275
4. .00001	**5.** .0505	**6.** 40
7. .085	**8.** .1903	**9.** .05722
10. .85	**11.** .431	**12.** .2347
13. 2.30125	**14.** 12	**15.** .00245
16. 16.005	**17.** .376	**18.** .17
19. .1101	**20.** .08297	**21.** .0375

Exercise 1: Decimal to Percent, page 14.

1. 8800%	**2.** 70%	**3.** 31%
4. 20.1%	**5.** 9%	**6.** 1.6%
7. 730%	**8.** 1832%	**9.** 54.1%
10. 671.2%	**11.** 140%	**12.** 61.8%
13. 21.5%	**14.** 17.8%	**15.** 2460%
16. 500%	**17.** 401%	**18.** .3%

Exercise 2: Decimal to Percent, page 15.

1. 3.8%	**2.** 1.4%	**3.** 4%
4. 2%	**5.** 47%	**6.** 85%
7. 64.3%	**8.** 30.7%	**9.** .5%

Exercise 1: Percent to Fraction, page 16.

1. $\frac{3}{4}$	**2.** $\frac{1}{50}$	**3.** $\frac{3}{50}$
4. $\frac{57}{100}$	**5.** $\frac{16}{25}$	**6.** $\frac{93}{100}$
7. $1\frac{1}{5}$	**8.** $\frac{22}{25}$	**9.** $2\frac{1}{2}$
10. 5	**11.** $14\frac{3}{10}$	**12.** $\frac{1}{20}$
13. $\frac{3}{5}$	**14.** $\frac{7}{10}$	**15.** $1\frac{1}{20}$
16. $3\frac{1}{4}$	**17.** $\frac{7}{10}$	**18.** 1

Exercise 2: Percent to Fraction, page 17.

1. $\frac{407}{100000}$	**2.** $\frac{601}{1000}$	**3.** $\frac{173}{1000}$
4. $\frac{549}{1000}$	**5.** $\frac{71}{400}$	**6.** $\frac{221}{400}$
7. $\frac{379}{400}$	**8.** $\frac{181}{250}$	**9.** $\frac{95}{400}$
10. $\frac{31}{200}$	**11.** $\frac{1}{200}$	**12.** $\frac{1}{150}$
13. $\frac{303}{500}$	**ı.** $\frac{49}{400}$	**15.** $\frac{131}{200}$
16. $\frac{351}{500}$	**17.** $\frac{11}{400}$	**18.** $\frac{1}{12}$
19. $\frac{27}{200}$	**20.** $\frac{61}{250}$	**21.** $\frac{41}{1000}$

Exercise 1: Fraction to Percent, page 18.

1. 49%	**2.** 13%	**3.** 3.2%
4. 50%	**5.** 75%	**6.** 60%
7. 45%	**8.** 32%	**9.** 10%
10. 67.5%	**11.** 1200%	**12.** 68%
13. 280%	**14.** 25.75%	**15.** 150%

Exercise 2: Fraction to Percent, page 19.

1. 19%	**2.** 39%	**3.** .73%
4. 175%	**5.** 360%	**6.** 112.5%
7. 33%	**8.** 400%	**9.** 18%
10. 3.18%	**11.** 67%	**12.** 133%
13. 37%	**14.** 18.75%	**15.** 25%
16. 360%	**17.** 83%	**18.** 12.5%
19. 414%	**20.** 944%	**21.** 765%

Review, pages 20–21.

A. Convert each percent to a decimal.

1. 726% = **7.26**   2. 3% = **.03**   3. 27.2% = **.272**

4. 6.99% = **.0699**   5. 12.5% = **.125**   6. .09% = **.0009**

7. 2275% = **22.75**   8. $24\frac{3}{5}$ % = **.246**   9. $3\frac{1}{8}$ % = **.03125**

B. Convert each decimal to a percent.

1. .07 = **7%**   2. .472 = **47.2%**   3. 7.6 = **760%**

4. 6 = **600%**   5. .0028 = **.28%**   6. .0876 = **8.76%**

7. .8 = **80%**   8. 15 = **1500%**   9. .72 = **72%**

C. Convert each percent to a fraction. Reduce to lowest terms if necessary.

1. 55% = $\frac{11}{20}$ 2. 800% = **8**   3. 7% = $\frac{7}{100}$

4. 90% = $\frac{9}{10}$ 5. $12\frac{1}{4}$ % = $\frac{49}{400}$ 6. $\frac{1}{2}$ % = $\frac{1}{200}$

7. 6.2% = $\frac{31}{500}$ 8. $5\frac{1}{10}$ % = $\frac{51}{1000}$ 9. 1.125% = $\frac{9}{800}$

D. Convert each fraction to a percent. Round any repeating decimal to the nearest hundredth.

1. $\frac{1}{3}$ = **33%**   2. $\frac{1}{2}$ = **50%**   3. $3\frac{3}{5}$ = **360%**

4. 12 = **1200%**   5. $\frac{8}{7}$ = **114%**   6. $10\frac{5}{6}$ = **1083%**

7. $\frac{11}{20}$ = **55%**   8. $\frac{21}{6}$ = **350%**   9. $\frac{.75}{100}$ = **.0075%**

E. Use equivalent forms to complete this table:

	Percent	Decimal	Fraction
1.	25%	.25	$\frac{1}{4}$
2.	4%	.04	$\frac{1}{25}$
3.	12.5%	.125	$\frac{1}{8}$
4.	32%	.32	$\frac{8}{25}$
5.	50%	.5	$\frac{1}{2}$
6.	80%	.8	$\frac{4}{5}$
7.	37%	.37	$\frac{37}{100}$
8.	64%	.64	$\frac{16}{25}$
9.	125%	1.25	$1\frac{1}{4}$
10.	.1%	.001	$\frac{1}{1000}$
11.	$7\frac{1}{2}$%	.075	$\frac{3}{40}$
12.	775%	7.75	$7\frac{3}{4}$
13.	3.5%	.035	$\frac{7}{20}$
14.	4.5%	.045	$\frac{9}{20}$
15.	6.25%	.0625	$\frac{1}{16}$
16.	167.5%	1.675	$1\frac{27}{40}$
17.	$\frac{3}{5}$%	.006	$\frac{3}{500}$
18.	800%	8	8
19.	74.5%	.745	$\frac{149}{200}$
20.	.6%	.006	$\frac{3}{500}$

Exercise 1: Finding the Part, page 22.

1. 40	**2.** 3.36	**3.** 2
4. 58.9	**5.** 21	**6.** 48
7. 28	**8.** 9.25	**9.** 124.8
10. 25	**11.** .045	**12.** 62.25

Exercise 2: Finding the Part, page 23.

1. 3.6	**2.** 13.5	**3.** 1.36
4. 2.73	**5.** .0156	**6.** 8.5
7. 9.3	**8.** 195	**9.** .576
10. .8442	**11.** 27.4	**12.** 25.875
13. .33	**14.** 13	

Exercise 1: Finding the Number, page 24.

1. 100	**2.** 150	**3.** 10
4. 53	**5.** 600	**6.** 100
7. 12.5	**8.** 67	**9.** 240
10. .60		

Exercise 2: Finding the Number, page 25.

1. $7.50	**2.** 125	**3.** 4400
4. 23.75	**5.** 70	**6.** 18.75
7. 32	**8.** $59	**9.** 55
10. 3000	**11.** 158	**12.** 36
13. 17	**14.** 72	**15.** $3275
16. $53		

Exercise 1: Finding the Percent, page 26.

1. 200%	**2.** 60%	**3.** 75%
4. 40%	**5.** 3%	**6.** 20%
7. 39%	**8.** 18.5%	**9.** 140%
10. 11.75 %		

Exercise 2: Finding the Percent, page 27.

1. 12.5%	**2.** 104%	**3.** 468.75%
4. 25%	**5.** 20%	**6.** 60%
7. 220%	**8.** 127%	**9.** 3.5%
10. 30%	**11.** 61%	**12.** 20%
13. 250%	**14.** 96%	**15.** 60%
16. 20%		

Exercise 1: Word Problems, page 29.

1. P = R x N , 1050 students   2. $R = \frac{P}{N}$, 80%

3. $N = \frac{P}{R}$, $180   4. $R = \frac{P}{N}$, 70%

5. $N = \frac{P}{R}$, $30   6. P = R x N , $.99

7. $R = \frac{P}{N}$, 65%   8. $N = \frac{P}{R}$, 720 students

9. P = R x N, $884   10. $R = \frac{P}{N}$, 60%

11. P = R x N, $22.80   12. $N = \frac{P}{R}$, $148

Review, pages 30–31.

A. Complete each of the following:

1. 27 is 75% of **36**

2. 29 is **25%** of 116

3. What percent of 7.5 is 3? **40%**

4. 12 is 12% of **100**

5. 17% of 190 = **32.3**

6. 45 is **60%** of 75

7. 8.48 is 53% of **16**

8. 15.8% of 72 = **11.376**

9. 68 is 200% of **34**

10. $62\frac{1}{2}$% of 96 = **60**

11. 56 is $87\frac{1}{2}$% of **64**

12. 18.36 is **25.5%** of 72

13. $37\frac{1}{2}$% of 88 = **33**

14. 475 is 190% of **250**

15. 124 is what % if 1240? **10%**

16. $66\frac{2}{3}$% of 96 is **64**

17. 17.02 is 46% of **37**

18. 52.8 is **70.4%** of 75

19. 15% of 15 is **2.25**

20. 53.2% of 29 equals **15.428**

B. Solve each word problem:

1. A mountain bike normally sells for $295. If the original price is reduced by $50.15, what is the percent of savings?
   17%

2. The sale price of a pair of shoes is $21. The sale price is 70% of the regular price. What is the regular price?
   $30.00

3. If an item normally costs $225 and it is offered at a 30% discount, how much will the discount be?
   $67.50

C. Solve the following problems:

1. 42.5% of 230 is what number?
   97.75

2. What number is 12.5% of 178?
   22.25

3. 88 is what percent of 64?
   137.5%

4. 1067.5 is 250% of what number?
   427

5. 63 is what percent of 300?
   21%

6. 386 is 19.3% of what number?
   2000

Exercise 1: Applying Percent, page 33.

1. $11.25, $33.75
2. $405
3. $3.50
4. $5.25, $29.75
5. $19.98
6. $98.88
7. $1348.60
8. $2084.20
9. $278.40, $649.60
10. $1000, $70

Post-Test, pages 34–35.

A. Supply equivalent values:

	Fraction	Decimal	Percent
1.	$\frac{1}{8}$	.125	12.5%
2.	$1\frac{1}{5}$	1.2	120%
3.	$\frac{11}{200}$	.055	5.5%
4.	$\frac{3}{500}$	.006	.6%
5.	$7\frac{9}{10}$	7.9	790%
6.	$\frac{1}{20}$	.05	5%
7.	$12\frac{1}{2}$	12.5	1250%
8.	$4\frac{3}{8}$	4.375	437.5%
9.	$\frac{7}{4}$	1.75	175%
10.	$\frac{1}{16}$	.0625	6.25%

B. Solve the following problems:

1. 125 is $33\frac{1}{3}$% of what number?
   375

2. What percent of 60 is 45?
   75%

3. 325% of 50 equals what number?
   162.5

4. $17\frac{1}{4}$% of 150 is what number?
   25.875

5. $12.75 is 60% of what number?
   $21.25

6. 2.5 is what percent of 40?
   6.25%

7. What number is 27% of 10?
   2.7

8. 80 is 128 % of what number?
   62.5

9. $6.25 is what percent of $25?
   25%

10. What number is .09% of 52?
   .0468

C. Word problems.

1. On a 50-question test, Danielle answered 78% of the questions correctly. How many questions did she answer correctly?
   39

2. Four pairs of sox cost $5.50. A 6% sales tax was added. How much was the purchase including the sales tax?
   $5.83

3. A local grocery store handed out 2470 coupons for a reduced price on detergent. 1482 coupons were returned. What percent of the coupons were returned?
   60%

4. A $45 appliance was purchased on sale at a 30% discount. What was the price of the appliance after the discount?
   $31.50

5. Of the employees at a large corporation, 14% filed their income tax reports late. If 168 people filed late tax reports, how many people are employed at the corporation?
   1200

6. Twenty-six out of 160 people who answered a newspaper ad were not qualified for the advertised job. What percent of those answering the ad were not qualified?
   16.25%

7. Daphne spent her $210 budget on Christmas gifts. This amount was 30% of her savings. How much was her savings?
   $700

8. What is a 15.5% tip on a $120 meal?
   $18.60

9. A pair of skis is priced at $185. Find the cost including a sales tax of 8%. Find the cost with a discount of 10% and a sales tax of 8%.
   $199.80, $179.82

10. The senior class raised 98% of its goal for graduation activities. It raised $10,878. How much was its goal?
   $11,100

11. The sales tax on a new car is $979.60. The car sold for $15,800. What is the sales tax rate?
   6.2%

12. Cecily saves 6% of her salary. If she saves $900 in one year, what is her annual salary?
   $15,000

39

Math Series

The Straight Forward Math Series

is systematic, first diagnosing skill levels, then *practice*, periodic *review*, and *testing*.

Blackline

GP-006 Addition
GP-012 Subtraction
GP-007 Multiplication
GP-013 Division
GP-039 Fractions
GP-083 Word Problems, Book 1
GP-042 Word Problems, Book 2

The Advanced Straight Forward Math Series

is a higher level system to diagnose, practice, review, and test skills.

Blackline

GP-015 Advanced Addition
GP-016 Advanced Subtraction
GP-017 Advanced Multiplication
GP-018 Advanced Division
GP-020 Advanced Decimals
GP-021 Advanced Fractions
GP-044 Mastery Tests
GP-025 Percent
GP-028 Pre-Algebra, Book 1
GP-029 Pre-Algebra, Book 2
GP-030 Pre-Geometry, Book 1
GP-031 Pre-Geometry, Book 2
GP-163 Pre-Algebra Companion

Upper Level Math Series

GP-104 Algebra, Book 1
GP-105 Algebra, Book 2
GP-045 Trigonometry
GP-054 Geometry
GP-053 Pre-Calculus
GP-064 Calculus AB, Vol. 1
GP-067 Calculus AB, Vol. 2

2 SIDED Self-Checking Math Puzzles

Each puzzle set contains 10 individual puzzles. Each six-inch puzzle is two-sided. One side contains basic math facts, the other side has a photograph. Each puzzle has its own clear plastic tray and lid.

Math problems are solved in the bottom tray (answer pieces are all the same shape). The lid is closed and the puzzle is turned over. If the photo is jumbled, the math facts have not been completed correctly.

GP-113 Addition Puzzles
GP-114 Subtraction Puzzles
GP-115 Multiplication Puzzles
GP-116 Division Puzzles
GP-122 Multiplication & Division Puzzles
GP-123 Money Puzzles

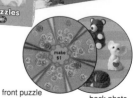

front puzzle   back photo